Our Beckoning Borders

Our Beckoning Borders

Illegal Immigration to America

Brent Ashabranner

Photographs by Paul Conklin

COBBLEHILL BOOKS

Dutton / New York

Library of Congress Cataloging-in-Publication Data

Ashabranner, Brent K., date
    Our beckoning borders: illegal immigration to America / Brent Ashabranner;
    photographs by Paul Conklin.
        p.   cm.
    Includes bibliographical references and index.
    Summary: Examines the problems connected with illegal immigration in the
    United States, from the perspectives of the immigrants themselves as well as
    from that of law enforcement officials.
    ISBN 0-525-65223-X
    1. United States—Emigration and immigration—Juvenile literature. 2. United
    States—Social conditions—1980—Juvenile literature. 3. Illegal aliens—United
    States—Juvenile literature. 4. Alien labor—United States—Juvenile literature.
    [1. Illegal aliens. 2. United States—Emigration and immigration.] I. Conklin,
    Paul, ill. II. Title.
    JV6455.A8915   1996   304.8' 73—dc20   95-45584   CIP AC

Published in the United States by Cobblehill Books,
an affiliate of Dutton Children's Books,
a division of Penguin Books USA Inc.,
375 Hudson Street, New York, New York 10014

Designed by Joy Taylor
Printed in the United States of America
First edition   10   9   8   7   6   5   4   3   2   1

For Ruth

Contents

Author's Note   *ix*

1. Illegal Immigration: How Great a Problem?   3
   The Hidden Face of Illegal Immigration: Visa Abusers   12
2. A Border Like No Other   15
   Maquiladoras   22
   Our Quiet Border   26
3. The Border Patrol   29
   Additional Facts about the Border Patrol   42
4. The Unwanted   45
   Guarding Our Shores Against Illegal Immigrants   56
   The Investigators   60
5. The Asylum Seekers   63
   The Border Watchers   72
6. Into a Strange Land   75
7. Illegal Immigration: Where Do We Go From Here?   83

United States Immigration Law and Selection System   89

A Note on Information Sources   91

Bibliography   93

Index   97

Author's Note

IN A SENSE Paul Conklin and I have been working on this book for fifteen years. When we researched and photographed *The New Americans* in 1981, we talked with illegal immigrants and Border Patrol agents in Texas. Three years later *Dark Harvest* took us over much of the United States interviewing migrant farmworkers, many of whom were undocumented aliens from Mexico. Our *Children of the Maya*, 1986, was about the tragic Guatemalan Indians who entered the United States illegally to escape persecution and in time were granted asylum. *The Vanishing Border* reported our 1987 journey along the entire length of our country's frontier with Mexico and our frequent talks with illegal immigrants. In 1993, this time working with my photographer daughter Jennifer Ashabranner, I wrote *Still a Nation of Immigrants* (Cobblehill/Dutton), again devoting some of the pages to illegal immigrants.

But when Paul and I started work on *Our Beckoning Borders*, we did our field research all over again: riding in Border Patrol vans along the Mexican border, visiting our border with Canada, going to cities with large numbers of illegal immigrants, and going to south Florida, still the target of boat people from Cuba, Haiti, and the Dominican Republic. I spent days gathering information from helpful officials of the U.S. Immigration and Naturalization Service (INS) in Washington, D.C.

According to an old cliché, the more things change, the more they stay the same. But the cliché does not fit illegal immigration at all well. One important thing has stayed the same: illegal immigrants are still entering the United States in large numbers. But other important things have changed and are still changing. The Border Patrol has more than doubled since our first acquaintance with it. The Immigration Reform and Control Act has made the hiring of illegal aliens a crime. Citizen concern has resulted in legislation such as California's Proposition 187. Concern about the number of Haitian and Cuban refugees has influenced our national policy toward both countries. Congress is pondering illegal immigration to an unprecedented degree. Paul and I wanted *Our Beckoning Borders* to be the most up-to-date look possible at this troubling national problem, and we believe it is.

In Chapter Two, I have adapted a few paragraphs from *The Vanishing Border* which seemed especially relevant.

A word on semantics: The term Hispanic is in general use today to refer to Americans of Spanish heritage. Some persons, however, prefer the term Latino or use it interchangeably with Hispanic. Many Mexican Americans refer to themselves as Chicanos. For the sake of consistency, I have used Hispanic throughout this book.

I would like to thank my daughter Melissa Ashabranner for invaluable research assistance and Paul's and my friend, Stephen

Chicoine, for help with contacts in Houston. As he has so many times before, Mark Franken of the U.S. Catholic Conference opened door after door for us in our inquiries; as always, we are grateful, Mark.

Brent Ashabranner

Our Beckoning Borders

Illegal aliens apprehended by the Border Patrol near Nogales.

1 Illegal Immigration: How Great a Problem?

EVERY MORNING at six o'clock Roberto leaves his shabby room in a Los Angeles boardinghouse and walks eight blocks to a street where mostly Hispanic men in work clothes have already begun to gather on the sidewalk. Like Roberto, they are illegal immigrants, and also like Roberto, they hope that a labor recruiter will come by and pick them for a day's work on a construction job. Hiring illegal aliens is against the law, but some employers are willing to take the risk because illegals will work for less pay and expect no job benefits beyond their daily pay.

With only a few years of elementary-school education, Roberto had never been able to find work in Hermosillo, Mexico, where he was born and grew up. He lived with his parents, who were very poor and who had eight other younger children. On his twenty-first birthday, Roberto decided to go to the United States. Some of his friends had gone already, and he had received a letter from one in Los Angeles who said there were jobs in that city. Roberto knew that he would never be approved as a regular immigrant, so he decided to cross the border illegally.

Roberto's mother gave him her blessing to leave Mexico; she also gave him a hundred dollars, all she could borrow from a money lender. Roberto went to Tijuana, a Mexican border city near San Diego, California. After a few days he located a "coyote," a person who guides or smuggles illegal aliens across the border. The coyote got him to San Diego, but Roberto had to give the man all of his money, keeping only enough for a bus ticket to Los Angeles.

For the past two years Roberto has begun almost every day standing on the same Los Angeles street hoping to be chosen for a job. He works two or three times a week and makes barely enough to live on, which he could not do in Mexico.

RINA is twenty-six, a native of the Central American country of El Salvador. After her husband died of cancer, Rina was unable to make a living for her four children and herself. Finally, she left her children with her sister and started for the United States. She traveled through Guatemala and Mexico, sometimes by bus, sometimes begging rides on trucks. Often she walked all night, sleeping a few hours beside the road.

Her journey took more than three weeks, but at last she reached the city of Nogales on the border. Nogales, Mexico, and Nogales, Arizona, are sister cities, and it was not hard to find a way to slip into Nogales on the U.S. side. But it was not easy to elude the U.S. Border Patrol. Rina was caught five times as she crossed into Arizona. Each time she convinced the Border Patrol agents that she was Mexican, and after she signed the voluntary return form, they sent her back across the border. Had the Border Patrol known she was from El Salvador, they could not

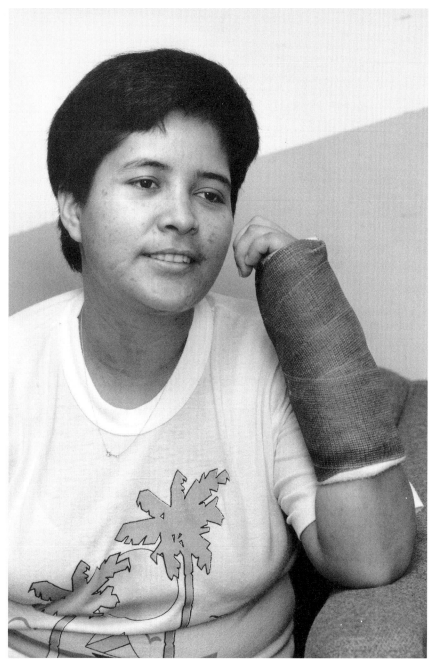

Rina

have returned her to Mexico; she would have been put in a detention camp for probable return to her own country.

When she had almost given up hope, a Mexican acquaintance who felt sorry for her gave Rina a school uniform to wear and a book to carry. She crossed the border once more and this time with her "disguise" escaped detection by the Border Patrol. Rina made her way to a Texas city and found work as a housecleaner and later as a live-in baby-sitter. Within a few months she was sending money back for her children and even beginning to save. Then one night she was robbed and beaten, her arm shattered. Now she is recovering in a Catholic shelter which does not ask whether a person is an illegal immigrant.

When her arm heals, Rina will try again to find work so that she can support her children in El Salvador.

ALEX was born in Mexico City into a family of nine children. His father is a factory worker. After Alex graduated from middle school, he wanted to go to trade school, but the family had no money to send him, and he was unable to earn money for school fees. So when Alex was sixteen, he went to Texas with a friend, crossing the Rio Grande at night near Matamoras, the sister city of Brownsville, Texas. Alex hitched rides to the Texas city where his brother lives; his brother is a legal resident of the United States, but that does not help Alex. He is still an illegal alien.

With his brother's assistance, Alex goes to school. He is a good student and will soon graduate from high school. Alex wants to stay in the United States, but as an illegal alien his chances of finding a steady job are poor. Still, he refuses to give up hope.

Alex with his friend Tomas (in hat), nineteen, who at age eleven was brought illegally into the United States by his father. Tomas has two sisters in Mexico whom he has not seen in seven years. "When I get a job, I will bring my sisters to live with me," says Tomas. "It is hard to live without love." But as an illegal alien, Tomas has little chance of getting an education or finding a steady job.

CYPRIAN is a young West African taxi driver. He is a good driver, cheerful, polite, and without a single accident to blemish his record. He has learned the city quite well and can take his customers to their destinations quickly. The most unusual thing about Cyprian is that he is not driving a taxi in his native city of Lagos, Nigeria. Instead, he drives his cab through the somewhat complicated streets of Washington, D.C.

Cyprian came to Washington four years ago to study at George Washington University. He had a passport and a student visa valid for two years. His government paid his expenses. At the end of two years Cyprian wanted to extend his study for another year, but his government said no. Even though his visa had expired and he was supposed to leave the country, Cyprian decided to stay in Washington. A friend gave him the taxi job, and he is taking night courses at George Washington. Cyprian knows that he is breaking the immigration law, but tries not to think about that. He likes America and has decided he wants to stay.

HUNDREDS of thousands of people like Roberto, Rina, and Alex come to the United States every year. They do not have a passport with an entry visa or any other legal border-crossing permit. They do not pass through an official port of entry as all persons who enter the country legally must do. In the language of the U.S. Immigration and Naturalization Service (INS), they are "undocumented." They are illegal aliens. Almost without exception, they are people who would have little chance of being approved as legal immigrants or would have to wait years for approval.

Thousands of people like Cyprian come to the United States legally each year but do not leave when their visas expire. They do not come on immigrant visas, but rather on temporary visas as tourists, students, or for business purposes. When their visas expire and they fail to leave the country, they become illegal aliens and are classified by the INS as "visa abusers." Visa abusers come from Africa, Asia, Europe, and every other part of the world.

The full dimensions of illegal immigration to the United States are hard to grasp because they involve countless stories of hardship and human need. But the cold, hard statistics of illegal immigration tell their own troubling story.

— An estimated 4 million illegal immigrants live in the United States today. This figure, as well as most of which follow, comes from the INS Statistics Division. Precise figures are impossible to obtain for the simple reason that illegal immigrants do not want to be counted.

— An estimated 300,000 illegal aliens settle permanently in the United States every year.

— The total number of illegal aliens entering the United States each year is much higher, between 1.5 million and 2.5 million. The majority are young single men. Most of these persons are called "sojourners." They come to do seasonal agricultural work or to visit family members living in the United States and then return home after a short stay. Many who come with the intention of staying permanently become discouraged and return home when they can't find work.

— More than 30 percent of all illegal immigrants in the United States are Mexicans.

— Over 3.4 million "deportable aliens" were apprehended crossing U.S. land borders or landing on U.S. shores during the years 1992-1994. Over 95 percent of those apprehended were persons who illegally crossed the U.S.-Mexican border.

— Regardless of where or how they entered the United States, illegal aliens from 170 different countries were apprehended in 1994.

THROUGHOUT its history the United States has received more immigrants from more countries than any other nation in the world. In recent years legal immigrants have totaled nearly 1 million annually. Over the centuries the United States has drawn richly from the cultural backgrounds of many immigrant groups — ideas, languages, customs, music, dance, food, dress — to forge a new culture, an American culture. We are truly a nation of immigrants.

But we are also a nation of laws. Americans who strongly support our national immigration program are troubled by the fact that millions of people enter, or try to enter, the United States illegally every year and that millions continue to break the law by staying here. In a *Washington Post* article entitled "Immigration: Making Americans," William J. Bennett is very positive about our legal immigration program. But in the article, Bennett, a former Secretary of Education, writes: "Illegal immigration is a very serious problem, and all Americans . . . are right to be upset and angry. Every sovereign nation has the right and the duty to control its borders."

Why is illegal immigration a serious problem?

The most obvious answer is that persons entering the country illegally and living here illegally show a disregard for the nation's laws. They may break no other laws once they are here; but they have broken the law by sneaking across the border, and they will remain lawbreakers simply by staying here. They will never be able to take part fully and responsibly in the life of the country because they do not belong here.

On a concrete level, numbers alone are at the heart of the problem, particularly their concentration in a few states.

According to INS statistics, 70 percent of all illegal aliens in the United States live in California, New York, Texas, Florida, and Illinois. Most illegal aliens are poor. Their high concentration in a few urban locations in those states causes problems of low-cost housing availability and strains health, educational, and other social and charitable services.

THE cost of fighting illegal immigration adds to an already overburdened national budget. The Border Patrol appropriation for 1994 was almost half a billion dollars and is certain to grow in future years. Illegal immigration has created a criminal industry in the manufacture and sale of fake Social Security cards, birth certificates, work permits, and other documents used to prove legal residence in the United States. The INS now spends over $300 million each year to combat document fraud, to enforce the law prohibiting employment of illegal immigrants, and to find and deport persons living illegally in the country.

Beyond these clearly defined problems are a number of serious questions. What has caused the upsurge of illegal immigration in recent years? Will it increase in the years ahead? Do illegal immigrants take jobs away from citizens and other legal residents of the United States? Do they contribute to a higher crime rate? Can we do a better job of finding and deporting people who are living in the United States illegally? Can our borders and shores be more effectively guarded than they now are? Are there approaches beyond law enforcement that can reduce illegal immigration?

In the pages ahead, we will look more closely at these problems and questions, most of which have no easy answers.

The Hidden Face of Illegal Immigration: Visa Abusers

WE THINK of illegal immigrants as people who clandestinely enter the United States by slipping past the Border Patrol on our border with Mexico or landing at night in small boats on the shores of south Florida. Many thousands do come in those ways; but according to INS figures, slightly more than half of the estimated 4 million illegal immigrants now living in the United States entered the country legally. Most arrived by air at Kennedy International Airport and at international airports in Los Angeles, Detroit, Houston, Miami, and other U.S. cities. Immigration inspectors in those ports of entry checked their passports, saw that they had proper tourist, business, or student visas, and doubtless waved them through with a smile as welcome visitors.

Every year about 20 million people come to the United States from all over the world for vacations, to visit relatives, to go to college, to do business, to take part in athletic events such as the Olympics in Atlanta. They come on temporary, nonimmigrant visas, usually for periods not exceeding three months but sometimes for several years in the case of students. Persons who apply for temporary visas at American embassies and consulates must have valid passports issued by the country of which they are citizens. They must show evidence that they have a genuine reason for their visits; they must show that they have the means to support themselves during their stays in the United States.

The great majority of visitors leave on schedule, but an average of about 150,000 a year do not. They remain in the United States after their visas have expired and are automatically classified as illegal aliens by the INS. Some of these visa abusers no doubt came to the United States with the intention of staying permanently, but for most the decision to remain probably was made after coming, perhaps influenced by family or friends in the United States. Regardless of motive, they are subject to immediate deportation if caught.

In fact, however, they are rarely caught. The INS has no specific program for finding and deporting visa abusers because such a program would be prohibitively expensive. In 1993, out of approximately 150,000 visa abusers, only about 600 were deported. If visa abusers do not run afoul of the law for some other reason, the chances are that they will be able to stay in the United States indefinitely. But they can never participate fully in the country's life. They cannot legally hold jobs; they cannot vote; they will live with the knowledge that they may be deported at any time.

Visa abuse — which occurs in less than 1 percent of all visas issued — is an unfortunate but probably inevitable price the United States pays for being an open, friendly country.

During the 1980s boat loads of Mexicans crossed the Rio Grande every day to reach El Paso during the "morning rush hour." This kind of casual border crossing has been stopped completely by the Border Patrol's Operation Hold the Line, begun in El Paso in 1993.

2 A Border Like No Other

THE UNITED STATES border with Mexico is 1,952 miles long and stretches from the Gulf of Mexico to the Pacific Ocean. The Rio Grande forms the entire boundary between Texas and Mexico. The river snakes its way south and east for 1,254 miles — almost two-thirds of the border's length — until it flows into the Gulf twenty miles east of Brownsville. Although it provides a clear, distinct, well-known division between Mexico and the United States, it is not much of a barrier. Small boats and swimmers find it little challenge; in some places, people wade across.

The border that separates Mexico from California, Arizona, and New Mexico has no river to define it. Most of its 698-mile length is marked by nothing more than a barbed-wire fence that in some places has fallen down. Only in urban areas where Mexican and U.S. cities exist side by side — Nogales, Mexico, and Nogales, Arizona, for example — do sturdier fences appear.

In this part of the West and Southwest the real barrier is the desert, stark mountains, and arid plains through which the border runs. *Jornada de la Muerte* — the Journey of Death — early

Spanish explorers called the border area in California. In Arizona and New Mexico the border crosses the inhospitable Sonoran and Chihuahuan deserts.

But in this seemingly harsh and uninviting terrain, human imagination, determination, and hard work have created cities, irrigated farms, citrus orchards, and cattle ranches on both sides of the border. And, in fact, deserts and mountains have proved to be no more a barrier to people on the move than the river that separates Texas and Mexico.

THERE are hundreds of borders between the many countries of the world. Some are longer than the border between the United States and Mexico. Our border with Canada is over twice as long, over three times as long when the Canadian-Alaskan border is included. But the U.S.-Mexican border is like no other border. Nowhere else on earth does a large, rich, highly industrialized country share such a long, open, unfortified, easily crossed border with a large, poor, less-developed country.

And an open border it is. While the Border Patrol apprehends more than a million illegal aliens a year, that many or more slip through the Border Patrol net. The true openness of the border, however, is to be found in another figure. In most recent years over 200 *million* legal border crossers from Mexico pass through our ports of entry into the United States — dayworkers, shoppers, tourists, immigrants. Mexicans visiting family members living in Texas and elsewhere in the United States account for millions of the border crossings. Many people make multiple entries, of course. The great border crossing points — the sister cities of Juárez and El Paso, Matamoros and Brownsville, the close-together cities of Tijuana and San Diego — form rivers of people flowing both ways. Smaller human rivers flow between the two countries in many places.

THE large-scale movement of people from Mexico to the United States is not new. Between 1910 and 1930, 685,000 Mexicans came to the United States as legal immigrants. Until 1965 there was no limit on the number of people from Mexico or other Western Hemisphere countries who could immigrate to the United States. There were immigration regulations, however: fees, health examinations, literacy tests, among other conditions. Large numbers of Mexicans entered the United States without paying the fees or taking the tests and thus were illegal immigrants. According to estimates at the time, illegal entrants outnumbered legal immigrants by a considerable margin.

The main motive for immigration during that period was the need for jobs. Many small Mexican farms had been absorbed by huge ranches, leaving farmers with no way to survive. Large numbers of Mexicans crossed the border illegally every year to become migrant farm laborers. Most returned to Mexico at the end of the harvest season, but many settled in California, Texas, and Florida.

During the 1960s and 1970s illegal immigration from Mexico to the United States dropped sharply and was considered only a minor problem. The reason for the decline was oil. Mexico, with an estimated 70 billion barrels of oil in a fuel-hungry world, was in a period of exciting growth and prosperity. Jobs

From these Juárez shacks, impoverished Mexicans can see the beckoning towers of El Paso.

During World War II and for twenty years after the war ended, almost 5 million Mexican men crossed the border to work on farms under the U.S.-Mexican agreement called the bracero *program. Pictured are the Mexican* bracero *workers near Stockton, California, in 1943. Millions of today's illegal immigrants from Mexico are following in the footsteps of their* bracero *fathers who came legally. (Library of Congress)*

were plentiful and prices of farm products good. But beginning in the early eighties, world oil prices fell, and Mexico has been in a severe economic slump ever since. Millions of Mexicans are unemployed or underemployed. In December, 1994, the Mexican government devalued the *peso*. The sharp fall in the value of the national currency has made farming a starvation business, and almost all other industries have been hard hit.

Infrared night telescopes help the Border Patrol see illegal border crossers at night.

Complicating the problem, Mexico has a booming population — soon to reach 100 million. Almost a million young men and women enter the job market every year.

Large-scale illegal migration of Mexicans across the border resumed in the early eighties and has continued unabated since that time. The apprehension of illegal border crossers in the San Diego Border Patrol Sector alone went from about 6,000 in 1965 to over 600,000 in 1986!

For millions of Mexicans who have lost jobs, who have never had a job, or who cannot make a living farming, there is no choice but to try to come to the United States, where they are not welcome, and to try to find work in a country where it is a crime for them to hold a job.

Maquiladoras

THE MEXICAN border cities are powerful people magnets. Every week thousands of Mexican job seekers arrive in Tijuana, Mexicali, Nogales, Juárez, Nuevo Laredo, Reynosa, and Matamoras. Many jobs in tourism and construction are to be had in those cities. But the greatest attraction for job-hungry people are the *maquiladoras*, factories that have been set up by U.S. firms in Mexican cities just over the border.

Maquiladoras are relatively new in U.S.-Mexico relations. When they started in 1966, there were only a few; now they are in every Mexican border city, over 2,200 of them, with new ones being built every month. The idea behind *maquiladoras* is simple. A U.S. company sends product parts duty free to its *maquiladora* "twin" in Mexico. Mexican workers in the counterpart company assemble the product, and it is shipped back to the parent company. A wide range of U.S. industries have *maquiladoras*; electronics, automotive, computer equipment are among the most important, but there are many others. U.S. corporations with *maquiladoras* can save millions of dollars in labor costs. A worker who costs a company $17 an hour in the United States may cost as little as $1 an hour in Mexico or even less. *Maquiladoras* are located in border cities to save transportation costs. The Mexican government encourages *maquiladoras* because they provide tens of thousands of jobs and bring much-needed dollars into the country.

But there is a darker side to the *maquiladora* story. Probably ten job seekers pour into the border cities for every position that

Lourdes, a Juárez slum dweller with her five-year-old daughter. Lourdes lives with her husband, two children, and two other adults in the shack in the background. It is made mainly of cardboard cartons. There is one water spigot for the entire area. Lourdes works for a maquiladora *that assembles thermostats; she earns 119* pesos *a week, about $30.*

is available in these U.S.-owned companies. Thousands of the hungry, desperate men and women who can't get work in the *maquiladoras* see the cities on the other side of the border — Calexico, Nogales, El Paso — and think of others beyond the border — San Diego, Los Angeles, Tucson, Houston — and make the decision to go to the United States.

There will be a border to cross, Border Patrol to elude, and no promise of a job beyond the border. But for people with nothing to lose, the road north is the only hope.

(Left) Nineteen-year-old Santos lives with his mother and brothers and sisters in the border city of Rio Bravo. Santos works for a maquiladora *owned by the Zenith corporation; his salary is $20 for a 45-hour work week. The family came from the interior of Mexico where work was impossible to find.*

Maria del Carmen's husband also works for Zenith and earns the same salary as Santos. Although their income is very small, Maria manages to dress her children well and buy a pretty, cheerful curtain for the door of their house.

Our Quiet Border

FROM THE Pacific coast of Washington to the Atlantic coast of Maine, the United States border with Canada is 3,987 miles long, which makes it slightly more than 2,000 miles longer than the U.S.-Mexican border. When Alaska's border with Canada is included, the total length of the boundary between the United States and Canada is 5,525 miles. In 1995, our long northern border was monitored by a force of 297 Border Patrol agents, almost 4,000 fewer than the Border Patrol strength on the Mexican border. The contrast in apprehensions is equally dramatic. In 1994, just over 1 million illegal aliens were apprehended crossing the Mexican border. Apprehensions on the Canadian border barely exceeded 13,000.

Despite the startling difference in numbers, our northern and southern borders have one thing in common: illegal aliens from many different countries cross both borders. Canadians, of course, make up the greatest number of apprehensions on the northern border, but illegal border crossers from many European countries — principally the United Kingdom, Poland, and other eastern European countries — are apprehended in most years. A few Australians, South Africans, and Middle Easterners are also regularly listed in the annual report of apprehensions. But, the Border Patrol notes, illegals do not cross the Canadian border in large groups as they often do the Mexican border. They usually attempt to cross alone or with a companion.

The Border Patrol is always on the alert for the smuggling of drugs, liquor, and tobacco (in the case of liquor and tobacco to avoid paying customs duty). Border Patrol agents do make apprehensions all along the border, but in most cases the smugglers are not coming from Canada. They are trying to get their contraband from the United States into Canada.

On the whole, however, the Canadian border is a quiet border. As Craig Jeffries, a Border Patrol agent assigned to the Havre, Montana, regional office, told us, "It's the most peaceful region in the country."

INS statistics support Agent Jeffries' assessment. In all of 1994, the Montana Sector recorded 1,294 apprehensions. The Border Patrol sector to the east, which includes North Dakota and Minnesota, recorded even fewer: 1,237. Together, the year's total for the two Canadian border sectors would be about the equivalent of two nights' work for the San Diego Sector.

Trails worn by nighttime illegal border crossers in the Chula Vista Border Patrol Sector near San Diego. In the background is Tijuana, Mexico.

3 The Border Patrol

On a warm March morning, Paul and I drove out of the Nogales Border Patrol headquarters with Senior Border Patrol Agent Steve McDonald at the wheel of an all-terrain Chevy Suburban. Most Border Patrol vans have a cage in back where illegal border crossers can be put when they are caught. Steve had chosen one that did not have a cage, figuring, I'm sure, that he would not arrest any illegals while he was showing a photographer and writer around. The shotgun rack in the front of the van was empty, again in deference to us, I assumed.

On the edge of town where the border was defined by five strands of rusting barbed wire, Steve pointed out a well-worn trail used by illegal border crossers. The trail led to a nearby housing development. "Our new strategy is to keep them out of town, where they can make it to a vehicle or safe house or lose themselves in the downtown crowd in two or three minutes," Steve said. "Out in the hills they have to walk twenty or thirty minutes in an unpopulated area, and we have a lot better chance to round them up."

This part of Arizona, called the Tucson Sector, was the latest border hotspot in the unending push of illegal immigrants to enter the United States. Paul and I had come to Nogales to see the Border Patrol's new strategy at work. Traditionally, the San Diego Sector of California and the El Paso Sector of Texas have been by far the busiest parts of the border for illegal crossings, but recently in those areas illegal entry had been sharply reduced. The Border Patrol — with newly appropriated Washington funds — had brought about the reduction by adding hundreds of additional agents, increasing air surveillance, installing powerful lights, and adding other sophisticated monitoring equipment. The El Paso effort, begun in September, 1993, was called Operation Blockade and later Operation Hold the Line; in California, underway in 1994, it was Operation Gatekeeper.

But with the slowdown in El Paso and San Diego illegal traffic came a sharp increase in Arizona border activity. Thousands of the Mexicans and other nationalities intent on entering the United States illegally simply shifted their efforts to a more vulnerable part of the long border. And their focus was Nogales, Arizona's chief border crossing with Mexico.

Now, however, Washington had given the Nogales Border Patrol the backing for its own new program, Operation Safeguard. Funds were provided for more ground sensors, additional aircraft, portable floodlights, and new night-vision devices. Most important, sixty-two new Border Patrol agents were assigned at the beginning of February, 1995, to join the ninety-eight agents already on duty in Nogales.

The results were dramatic. In February, the Border Patrol arrested 17,579 illegal aliens in and around Nogales, a record number of arrests by a wide margin. By comparison, 3,577 arrests had been made in Nogales in February of the previous year. The startling increase in arrests meant two things: illegal aliens were converging on Nogales in record numbers; the Border Patrol was catching them in record numbers.

"How many don't you catch?" I asked Steve. "How many get through?"

"There's no way to know," Steve said. "But even if they get through, we may catch them before they get out of our territory. We stopped a van this morning on Interstate 19 with twenty-eight illegals in it. Think of the logistics of getting that many people across the border at the same time!"

We were well outside Nogales now, and I found myself listening to the chatter on the van's two-way radio.

"Three of them working their way west."

"There's a solo up there hiding in the bushes."

When I asked Steve about the radio chatter, he said, "Our lookouts in the high places keep the closest units alerted."

We bounced over rutted dirt tracks that the Border Patrol calls drag roads. The rolling hills, partially covered with mesquite, had eroded into washes, wrinkled and fissured into gullies and ridges. Steve called some of the places by their names: Smugglers Gulch, Bar KS Wash, Kimmer Wash.

We stopped at Kimmer Wash, and Steve pointed out tracks made by an illegal border crosser. The *huaraches* (sandals) he wore had been made of cut-up car tires. Steve studied the tracks. "He's a big fellow. Look at the size of them. He's from down south, and he's been through here recently. You can tell they're new tracks because they 'shine up.' They're brighter than the rest of the ground."

Over the past few years, Paul and I had met several Border

Cutting sign. A Border Patrol agent from the Tacna Station east of Yuma, Arizona, looks for tracks of illegal border crossers. Agents skilled in tracking sometimes save illegal aliens lost and dying from thirst in the desert.

Patrol agents who were good at "cutting sign," tracking illegal border crossers by following their footprints and looking for other signs such as a cigarette butt, an empty tomato can, a broken branch on a bush, a mashed-down place where the person might have slept or rested. In a number of cases Border Patrol agents have tracked illegals who were hopelessly lost in the desert and saved them from dying of thirst.

A few minutes later Steve stopped again, and we got out. "It's Grand Central Station here," he said, pointing to a jumble of footprints. "We've been running into groups of as many as a hundred out here. See that water tank over on that hill. It's their landmark. They guide on it. We've convinced most of them that if they come over the fence, they'll be caught. So now they're trying other things — crossing out here in the hills, crossing at night."

The fence Steve spoke of is a 10-foot high border fence made of surplus military runway mats. It runs through the town of Nogales, separating it from Nogales, Mexico. The fence was put up laboriously by the Border Patrol over a period of months. In April, 1995, the Army Corps of Engineers extended it to an overall length of two-and-a-quarter miles. The high, olive-drab fence is not a pretty sight. Some Americans have called it an eyesore and a bad symbol for two friendly countries. Some Mexicans have called it insulting. But it does make illegal entry into Nogales, Arizona, much, much harder.

The fence does not discourage all illegal border crossers, however. As we drove back into town, I became aware of radio chatter again.

"Another one coming over the fence."

"Five guys going up the trail."

Illegal aliens apprehended after going around the 10-foot high Nogales border fence.

"Bike patrol, stay where you are. They'll run right into you."

Steve had obviously been listening to the radio before I heard anything because he already had the van headed for the action. Nogales is built on a series of hills with ravines and washes between them. Steve drove the van expertly through the narrow, twisting streets of a residential area, and soon we were at a place called Trickey Wash. Two Border Patrol vans were there when we arrived.

In not more than a minute six illegals, all young men, walked up the well-worn trail out of Trickey Wash, two Border Patrol agents behind them. The illegals were told to put their hands on one of the vans, searched quickly, and put into the cages in the backs of the vans. The whole operation couldn't have taken more than five minutes.

"They're all Mexicans," Steve said. "They'll sign voluntary return forms, and we'll put them back across the border. With them it's '*siempre mañana*.' There's always tomorrow. Some of them may be back across in an hour."

I was curious about something and said to Steve, "None of them had a suitcase or a backpack or was carrying anything."

"There's a Border Patrol saying," Steve answered, "that they're wearing their suitcases. They may have brought a suitcase or a bag, but they don't want to be hampered by it when they cross the border. So they put on as many clothes as they can, two pairs of pants, two shirts, two or three pairs of socks, anything they can, no matter how hot it is, and throw away their bags."

At headquarters we walked in on some excitement. A Border Patrol unit had just arrived with a dozen or so small bales of marijuana wrapped in black plastic. Agents had found the marijuana cached somewhere in the hills, but I couldn't get details

Illegal aliens caught in Trickey Wash, Nogales, are searched for weapons. The Border Patrol agent in shorts is a member of the bike unit.

because, as one agent said, it was an ongoing investigation. I watched them weigh the bales, and the total was 700 pounds. The street price of marijuana, I was told, was $800 a pound, which meant that the Border Patrol had taken a tidy half million dollars out of the hands of smugglers that day.

Seeing all of that black-wrapped narcotic reminded me that Border Patrol agents don't spend all of their time apprehending illegal border crossers.

THE next morning Paul and I went out again, this time with Supervisory Border Patrol Agent David Guttierez, a seventeen-year veteran of the Border Patrol. Dave was born in Nogales and had spent much of his boyhood here before his family moved to El Paso. He had been back as a member of the Border Patrol for several years.

We drove out into the hills again. Dave showed us well-worn trails frequently used by illegal border crossers. Seismic sensors were buried along the trails. If anyone stepped on one, a signal would be sent to the central monitoring room at Border Patrol headquarters, and the nearest agents would be alerted via the two-way radio. Dave pointed out one of the fourteen TV towers in the Nogales area that feed border pictures back to the monitoring room. On the crest of a hill I saw a parked Border Patrol van. An agent with binoculars stood in front of it, surveying the border, the washes, the roads, and trails. He or his replacement would be there around the clock.

"I don't see how anyone gets through," I said.

"Numbers," Dave answered, "and they never stop coming."

Seven hundred pounds of marijuana confiscated by Border Patrol agents near Nogales.

As we drove, Dave talked about many things: the coyotes, smugglers of human beings, who charged as much as $200 to get an illegal alien to Phoenix, as much as $1,500 to get one to Chicago. There are "drop houses" in Tucson and Phoenix where illegals can stay for a price until arrangements are made to get them to somewhere else in the United States where they want to go.

Steve McDonald had told us about illegal border-crossing groups as large as a hundred. Dave added something to that. Sometimes now drug smugglers time their border crossing with big groups, lagging a half hour or so behind. If Border Patrol agents intercept the big group, they have so much work on their hands that the drug smugglers have a better chance to get through. And some of the illegal aliens will probably get away in the confusion.

"In my time," Dave said, "border violence has become much greater. There is too much money involved now in the smuggling of drugs and people. Yes, it's a dangerous place."

Dave should know. One year ago on this exact day, he had been shot in the stomach while he was on patrol duty. Today he was wearing a bulletproof vest under his shirt.

"Kind of an anniversary reminder," he said with a smile.

Suddenly, I was aware of increased radio talk, and, as Steve had done yesterday, Dave responded. We drove to a Nogales outskirt housing area called West International, which backs up to the border. The 10-foot fence comes to an end here. As we reached a spot near the fence, I saw that several other Border Patrol vans had already arrived, as well as two members of the Border Patrol bike squad. On the highest hill in the area a Border Patrol agent stood beside his van, clearly directing the operation. Just as we arrived a helicopter appeared and hovered overhead.

We were not there over five minutes before — just as yesterday — a line of illegal border crossers appeared, shepherded by Border Patrol agents. The illegals had skirted the big fence only to be stopped before they had been in the United States more than a minute or two. They were quickly put in the Border Patrol van cages and were on their way back to Mexico or to detention if they were not Mexicans.

On our way back to headquarters, the radio started again, a lookout pinpointing two illegals who had just gone over the fence.

"Does it ever stop?" I asked.

"Not anymore," Dave said.

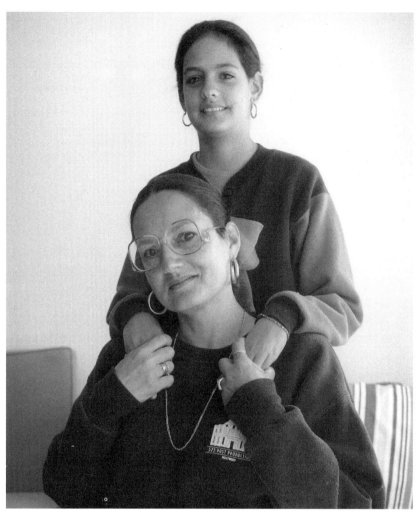

Norma, with her twelve-year-old daughter Aranzazu, is evidence that not all undocumented immigrants are uneducated and untrained. She was educated in the United States and at the University of Guadalajara, where she met her husband, an import-export business-man. When devaluation of the peso *destroyed their business in Juárez, Norma, her husband, and their three children came to Texas, entering on the husband's visa. They now live in a dilapidated house without heat or running water. But they plan to stay permanently in the United States and hope to gain resident status.*

THE Border Patrol agents Paul and I have met from California to Texas take their work seriously and do their job with dedication and courage. But we have yet to meet an agent who believes that the problem of illegal immigration can be solved solely by apprehending people who cross the border illegally, no matter how many agents are hired and how much high-tech surveillance equipment is installed.

Kevin Oaks, a Nogales Border Patrol agent, seemed to voice the thoughts of many of his fellow agents when he told a *Washington Post* reporter: "You can't stop the alien problem by putting up fences and increasing patrols. It's a tactic to slow them down and make them move somewhere else, but it's no miracle solution."

Kevin Oaks is right. The border is too long and the press of desperate people too constant to completely solve the problem through arrests. "But we can keep the lid on," a Border Patrol agent said to me in California. "That's our job."

Additional Facts about the Border Patrol

THE UNITED STATES Border Patrol was established on July 1, 1924, to help enforce immigration laws passed in 1921 and 1924. Those laws set strict new limits on the number of immigrants who could legally enter the country each year. The primary mission of the Border Patrol has remained unchanged since its establishment: to prevent the unlawful entry of undocumented aliens into the United States across the country's land borders and to apprehend those who succeed in crossing. In 1994, the Border Patrol apprehended 1,031,270 illegal aliens and seized 18,239 vehicles carrying illegal aliens; 139 boats and airplanes were also confiscated. With the increase in drug smuggling, the Border Patrol is the principal drug interdicting agency along our land borders. (The Border Patrol and the Coast Guard use the word "interdict" frequently to describe their work. They use it in the military sense of destroying, damaging, hampering, or capturing the enemy.)

In mid-1995, a total of 4,640 Border Patrol agents were in service. Of this total, over 4,000 were assigned to the U.S.-Mexican border. An additional 400 Border Patrol agents were to be recruited during the second half of 1995, most to be assigned to our southern border.

The Border Patrol is a highly mobile and uniformed arm of the Immigration and Naturalization Service under the Department of Justice. It is governed by Civil Service regulations. Border Patrol agents must be U.S. citizens. Applicants for Border Patrol service are prescreened by a questionnaire and

Ken Knowles, one of the nine-member Nogales Border Patrol bike unit. Their bikes are the latest and best in mountain bike equipment. "I love it," says Ken. "There's something doing every minute."

selected through written and oral examinations and a thorough background check.

Persons selected go through an eighteen-week training program at the Federal Law Enforcement Training Center at Brunswick, Georgia. The program includes a course in immigration law and intensive training in the Spanish language. Physical education, use of firearms, and defensive driving are parts of the training.

Upon successful completion of the training program, the graduate becomes a Journeyman Border Patrol Agent. Successive grades within the service are Border Patrol Agent, Senior Border Patrol Agent, and Supervisory Border Patrol Agent. About 3 percent of all Border Patrol agents are women. The Border Patrol is trying to increase this percentage by encouraging more women to apply for service in the organization.

A Juárez slum. People without hope have nothing to lose by illegal immigration to the United States.

4 The Unwanted

Paul and I have seldom been with a Border Patrol agent who did not express some sympathy for the illegal border crossers they catch and return to Mexico or put in detention centers. Talking about the terrible economic situation in Mexico that is driving people across the border, Steve McDonald said, "If I were starving down there, I'd do the same thing. You can't blame them."

And during our morning with Dave Guttierez, he remarked, "They are poor, decent people. You have to feel sorry for them."

The agents never let feelings get in the way of doing their job, but the feelings are there. Recently retired Senior Border Patrol Agent H.M. "Mike" Calvert spent much of his career apprehending illegal aliens. Mike is a no-nonsense, unsentimental guy; Paul and I have been with him when he arrested illegals on the streets of El Paso and when he was tracking them in the hills outside the city. But I remember Mike saying to us, "Ninety-five out of a hundred of these illegals aren't bad people. They just want one thing — to get a job, work hard, and send money home to help their poor families. If they could make a decent living in Mexico, there wouldn't be any illegal alien problem, at least not much of one."

I'm sure Mike is right. The need to work, the hunger for a job drives them. Paul and I have been with migrant farmworkers, most of them illegal aliens, while they were picking apples in New York, tomatoes on the Eastern Shore of Maryland, cucumbers and oranges in Florida. Their days in the fields and orchards are long, and they work with a steady intensity because they are paid only for the baskets they fill. When a job is finished, their only hope is that their delapidated cars and trucks will get them to the next harvest.

We have talked with illegal immigrants in California, Texas, Washington, D.C., and other places. Many were holding two jobs, sometimes three, loading trucks or doing yard work by day, washing dishes or cleaning office buildings at night.

Yes, they want to work.

And I think Mike is right that the great majority of them are not bad people. Out of 4 million illegal immigrants, some bad ones are going to show up; some will commit crimes, both petty and serious. Petty crime in cities on or near the border is sometimes more prevalent than in other places; but to the extent that illegal aliens contribute to it, they are mostly young men who sneak over the border for a few hours then return to where they came from. They are not immigrants who intend to stay.

In 1980, Fidel Castro emptied Cuba's jails and sent thousands of lawbreakers to Florida mixed in with over 100,000 refugees who were allowed to leave Cuba from the port of Mariel and head for south Florida in small boats. Many of those taken from jail were people who had been imprisoned because their political view differed from Castro's, but hundreds of dangerous real criminals were among the "Marielitos." The INS and other law enforcement agencies identified and arrested about 1,500 of these serious criminals, and they were put in federal prisons.

When looked at in the context of more than 120,000 Mariel boat people who arrived in 1980, the number who have not been successfully resettled is very small. As *The Washington Post* said in an editorial in 1982: "Fidel Castro undoubtedly thought he would embarrass and discredit our government by unloading his undesirables on the beach of Key West. He must have been disappointed. Americans have accorded the migrants both charity and justice."

Except for the Mariel episode, no research has shown that, as a group, illegal immigrants have a higher crime rate than legal immigrants or native-born citizens. So if illegal aliens want to work and they do not represent an unusual crime risk, what is the problem?

The problem, quite simply put, is that there is in the United States a pervasive feeling of ill will toward illegal immigrants. In some of the states with the largest illegal immigrant populations, the resentment is intense and sometimes front-page news. In Florida in 1994, illegal immigration was either first or second on a list of voter concerns in two newspaper polls. On November 8, 1994, California voters approved Proposition 187, an initiative that would deny schooling, nonemergency health care, and other government benefits to the state's 1.5 million illegal immigrants. (Proposition 187 cannot be put into effect until state and federal courts have ruled on whether it is constitutional.)

Congress has consistently reflected voter feelings about illegal immigrants. Members of both the Senate and the House of Representatives differ strongly on how many legal immigrants should be admitted to the country, but they are unanimous in opposing illegal immigration. Massachusetts Senator Edward Kennedy, for example, has always been a steadfast supporter of a liberal immigration policy, but in a statement in 1995 he took pains to show his disapproval of illegal immigration.

"I particularly support the increase in the Border Patrol," he said, "and in workplace enforcement of our immigration laws."

By "workplace enforcement" Senator Kennedy was referring to enforcing the law against hiring undocumented aliens. In 1986, Congress passed the Immigration Reform and Control Act (IRCA). The law had many provisions, but two were by far the most important. One part of the law gave amnesty to illegal aliens who had entered the United States before 1982 and allowed them to apply for permanent legal residence; in time, they could apply for citizenship. Under this amnesty almost 2 million illegal aliens, most of them Mexicans, became legal residents of the United States.

The other key provision of IRCA made the hiring of anyone who could not prove legal U.S. residence a crime. Employers who failed to ask a prospective employee for an Alien Registration card (the so-called green card), Social Security card, birth certificate, or other proof of legal residence could be fined or even put in jail. Employers, however, were not required to check the authenticity of these documents, which would have been impossibly complicated and time-consuming.

Congress believed that when people of other countries knew they could not get a job if they entered the country illegally, they would stop coming. When illegal immigration declined for several months after passage of IRCA, the Congressional lawmakers seemed to be right. But soon the illegal flow resumed and grew

Mario Casteneda was one of the almost 2 million illegal immigrants given amnesty by the Immigration Reform and Control Act of 1986. Now a productive member of the work force in northern Virginia, he plans to apply soon for U.S. citizenship. (Jennifer Ashabranner)

49

to previous levels. The manufacture of fake documents to prove legal residence became a booming business. A study in Houston showed that two out of every three illegal aliens in the survey had purchased fake identification documents for as little as $20.

Other problems with enforcing the law were soon apparent. Agricultural work and low-paying service jobs and day labor were hard for INS inspectors to monitor. In many cases illegal aliens worked for friends and family members who were legal U.S. residents. In some instances illegals went into business for themselves as vendors or craftsmen.

THE general widespread disapproval of illegal immigrants is abundantly clear, but why *specifically* do so many Americans resent and even fear them?

One specific reason, in fact, stems from a vague fear that the country is being overrun with illegal aliens. Scare headlines and frightening language in newspaper stories feed this fear. Here are examples: "The stream of illegal aliens pouring into the United States has become a torrent . . . the Border Patrol is inundated." *(Christian Science Monitor)*; "If in the future a sudden . . . increase in the human flow overwhelms the Border Patrol . . ." and ". . . the world's surging tides of excess people . . ." (*The Washington Post*). Other media phrases refer to "the hordes of illegal Mexican aliens" and call the border situation "totally out of control."

Journalists understandably want to make their points with dramatic language. But words and phrases like "overwhelm," "hordes," and "totally out of control" are red flags that stay in readers' minds and arouse fears of chaos and social breakdown.

In much recent travel with the Border Patrol, Paul and I never had a sense that they felt overwhelmed or inundated. I must say, however, that the Border Patrol does not add to the public peace of mind by giving its daily work such names as "Operation Blockade" and "Operation Hold the Line."

Commenting on public unease about illegal immigration, Bill Ong Hing, an immigration specialist at Stanford University, says, "There is a sense of loss of control. I don't think we have [lost control], but there's a sense of that."

A MUCH more specific cause of public resentment in areas with large numbers of illegal immigrants is the belief and some evidence that they do not pay their fair share of taxes and are a burden on public resources. This resentment undoubtedly fueled the passage of Proposition 187 in California, where an estimated 300,000 to 400,000 children of illegal immigrant parents are enrolled in public schools.

Contrary to popular belief, illegal immigrants are not eligible for many public services, including welfare, unemployment insurance, and most tax-paid health-care services. Programs which are available to them are Medicaid (for emergency services only); nutritional assistance to women, infants, and children; school lunches and breakfasts. Most important, the Supreme Court decided in 1982 that all children in the United States, including children of illegal immigrant parents, are entitled to public education. The court decided that the children are not in the United States of their own free will and should not be deprived of education because their parents are illegal aliens.

A study by the INS in the 1980s calculated that each 1 mil-

Hilde, an undocumented woman from Mexico, lives in an El Paso suburb with her two young daughters, cleaning houses to support them. "I have reached some of my goals," she says. "I am learning English. I will get my papers for legal residence. I am stubborn. People call me a little mule."

lion illegal aliens cost federal, state, and local governments $2.25 billion a year in education, law enforcement, health, and other benefits. Taxes paid by each 1 million illegals (principally federal and state income taxes and sales taxes on goods purchased) were estimated to be $995 million, leaving a net cost of $1.25 billion for each 1 million illegal aliens. Since California has at least 1.5 million illegal immigrants, their cost to state, county, and city governments would be close to $2 billion a year. This is a significant extra load for the citizens and other legal resident taxpayers of California to shoulder.

With an illegal immigrant population of about 350,000, Florida's problems are smaller than those of California. Still, according to Florida Governor Lawton Chiles, illegal immigrants have cost his state $1.5 billion since 1988. Florida sued the federal government for that amount, contending that immigration is a federal responsibility. Florida lost the case, but Florida citizens were made sharply aware of the cost of illegal immigration to them.

Do ILLEGAL immigrants take jobs away from U.S. citizens and other legal residents? Many people believe they do, and that belief probably causes more resentment of illegals than anything else. Studies do not show any clear impact of undocumented workers on the labor market. Most of those who find work hold only low-level, low-paying construction, hotel, restaurant, manufacturing, and domestic service jobs. Some labor observers contend that illegal aliens fill only jobs that Americans won't take. Agriculture is probably the industry most dependent on illegal workers. An estimated 20 to 40 percent of the 2 to 3 million agricultural workers are undocumented.

But despite what studies show, in difficult economic times Americans looking for jobs must wonder about the hundreds of thousands of work-hungry people crossing the border every year. A 1994-95 INS survey of 500 Arizona companies revealed that out of 50,000 employees, about 5,000 — about one in ten — were illegal immigrants using fraudulent employment documents. It is hard to convince many unemployed Americans that illegal newcomers don't increase competition in the job market and that they don't drive down pay scales.

THE general resentment of illegal immigrants has some exceptions. Many families in the United States today are "mixed" in that they are made up of some combination of native-born citizens, naturalized citizens, legal immigrant noncitizens, and illegal immigrants. This is particularly true in California, Arizona, New Mexico, and Texas where families have lived on both sides of the border for generations and have visited each other back and forth. In numerous cases, undocumented family members from Mexico or Central American countries have made the decision to remain with family living in the United States.

The same is true of visa abusers from all parts of the world. They come to visit family members who have immigrated legally to the United States, but they do not return when their temporary visas expire. They become a part of their U.S. relatives' family. Many of them hope to become legal residents, and some, with the sponsorship of the family in the United States, achieve their ambition.

Americans who do not live on the U.S.-Mexican border can

hardly understand how closely families on both sides are linked, indeed how closely all border people are linked. A few years ago when Paul and I were gathering material for our book *The Vanishing Border*, we talked to Pablo Salcido, a Mexican American who was then director of the Office of Development for the city of El Paso. Pablo tried to explain the border closeness to us.

"Both sides of the river are tied together in so many ways," he said. "We have cousins, uncles, aunts who live in Chihuahua. I can't pretend they don't exist. We can't talk about Mexican and U.S. problems as though they are separate — not here, we can't. It's *our* health, *our* economy, *our* school system, *our* employment, *our* acquifer. We drink the same water!"

Some U.S. senators and representatives now favor reducing the number of legal immigrants the United States admits each year, in part because of the continued increase in illegal immigrants. Without doubt, inadequately controlled illegal immigration will have a negative effect on legal immigration. Ron Sanders, Chief Border Patrol Agent for the Tucson Sector, recently wrote about this inevitable relationship:

"Legal immigration, when properly legislated and enforced, can have a positive impact on our economic and social structures as we approach the next century.

"If we fail to control illegal immigration, legal immigration will no longer have the meaning that is intended by statute for those who play by the legal rules implemented by our legislative branch of government.

"If we fail to control our borders, the beacon of hope that has shone so brightly during the past century could lose its sparkle for future generations of immigrants."

Guarding Our Shores Against Illegal Immigrants

THE COAST GUARD is the primary federal agency for enforcing United States law at sea. As such, one of its responsibilities is to prevent people of other countries from entering the United States illegally by sea. To carry out its many duties, which include maritime law enforcement, maritime safety, environmental protection, and national security, the Coast Guard has a fleet of forty-five high-endurance and medium-endurance cutters plus hundreds of smaller boats for patrol, search, and rescue. The Coast Guard also has over two hundred aircraft for search and rescue and other purposes.

For years the Coast Guard has intercepted thousands of boats and rafts crammed with Cubans and Haitians hoping to reach Key West or other beaches on the Atlantic coast of south Florida. Until recently Coast Guard cutters brought the desperate voyagers they intercepted to Florida where they were interned. After immigration hearings, most Haitians were deported, although during the repressive regimes of "Papa Doc" François Duvalier and his son "Baby Doc" Jean-Claude Duvalier some Haitians were given refugee status and allowed to stay in the United States.

The treatment accorded Cubans was entirely different. Under Fidel Castro, Cuba became a Communist country in 1959 — the only Communist country in Latin America and a firm ally of the Soviet Union. A mass exodus of Cubans escaping the

Communist regime began in 1960. During the next three decades almost a million people fled Cuba in unseaworthy small boats and rafts. Thousands would have drowned except for Coast Guard rescue. Since they were escaping from a Communist country, the U.S. government gave almost all Cubans refugee status. They became legal residents, and hundreds of thousands later became naturalized U.S. citizens.

In 1994, the treatment of Cubans and Haitians changed dramatically. Already concerned about the growing number of illegal aliens crossing the U.S.-Mexican border, the Clinton administration was suddenly faced with a sharp increase of boat people from Cuba and Haiti. In a two-month period during the summer of 1994, the Coast Guard intercepted 20,000 boat people from Haiti and over 32,000 from Cuba. U.S. government officials quickly developed a new policy. The Haitians were interned at the U.S. naval base in Guantánamo Bay, Cuba, and given "safe haven" status. After U.S. military intervention in Haiti in September, 1994, and the return of Haitian President Jean-Bertrand Aristide to power, the Haitians at Guantánamo Bay were returned to Haiti. About 16,000 returned voluntarily; the rest were returned forcibly.

In a complete policy turnaround, the 32,000 Cubans intercepted in the summer of 1994 were also interned at Guantánamo Bay. For the first time in over thirty years Cuban

A Coast Guard cutter intercepts a Haitian boat trying to reach the coast of south Florida. During the summer of 1994, 20,000 Haitians fleeing their troubled homeland in small boats were intercepted and taken to the U.S. naval base in Guantánamo, Cuba, for detention.

U.S. Coast Guard photographs

asylum seekers were not given almost automatic refugee status. Also for the first time the U.S. and Cuban governments tried to reach an agreement: the United States would increase immigration visas available to Cubans to 20,000 a year and Castro's government would try to prevent refugees from leaving Cuba in boats for the United States. By the summer of 1995, some of the Cubans held at Guantánamo Bay had been allowed to come to the United States, and a smaller number returned to Cuba. Most were still held at the U.S. naval base with no decision about their future in sight.

But as a result of U.S. intervention in Haiti and the potential policy change toward Cuba — still hotly debated in the United States — the flow of boat people from the Caribbean has become a trickle.

Except for the Caribbean migrants, the Coast Guard has never had a serious problem with illegal aliens trying to enter the United States from the sea. In recent years, however, a growing number of young men from the People's Republic of China have been apprehended attempting illegal entry. Most of them arrive on the West Coast in tramp steamers; their passage has been arranged, usually at a cost of thousands of dollars, by professional smugglers. In the first six months of 1995, the Coast Guard "for probable cause" boarded a number of ships arriving in West Coast waters and apprehended more than 450 Chinese intending undocumented entry into the United States.

Coast Guard crew members who serve aboard ships concerned with the interdiction of illegal aliens receive special training at the Maritime Law Enforcement School in Yorktown, Virginia.

The Investigators

TODAY, over 2,000 INS investigators are on the trail of document fraud, particularly in the states where the abuse is greatest: California, Arizona, Texas, New York, and New Jersey. In California alone in 1993 and 1994, investigators seized half a million counterfeit documents, mainly Alien Registration cards (the so-called green card which is the exclusive form of registration for lawful permanent residents), Social Security cards, and birth certificates. In those same years INS investigators obtained 1,249 criminal convictions against defendents for immigration-documents fraud offenses.

In 1995, INS investigators capped a two-year "sting" operation by arresting a California man they identified as the "godfather" of illegal immigration with a counterfeit documents network in six states bringing in over $1 million a month. The ring was selling fake green cards, Social Security cards, and driver's licenses for between $130 and $180 each. The INS has also broken up two counterfeit document rings in Newark, New Jersey, and one in New York City.

In 1994 and 1995, the INS Forensic Document Laboratory helped in the conviction of 138 counterfeiters of immigration documents. In those same years, the laboratory also trained more than 5,000 persons in different parts of the country in the detection of fraudulent immigration documents.

President Clinton has directed the INS and the Social Security Administration to develop an employment verification system that will make the use of fake documents harder. The two agencies are working on several pilot projects. Most promising is a computerized database combining Social Security and INS records. A telephone system would then be developed to allow employers to verify the legal status of a prospective employee. There is general agreement that inventing a foolproof system will be difficult, but many experts agree that a good system of proving a job applicant's legal status is the best way to reduce illegal immigration. Such a system, with proper safeguards, can also protect legal job applicants who might be discriminated against because they "look foreign" or have foreign-sounding names.

The INS wants to add several hundred more investigators for better enforcement of the law against hiring illegal aliens. The additional investigators will make possible more visits to factories and other workplaces to check the documents of employees and to make sure employers are not hiring workers without documents.

In asking for the additional help, INS Commissioner Doris M. Meissner said, "You can't do it all on the border unless you bolster it with enforcement in the interior."

A Border Patrol agent talks with two Guatemalans apprehended near San Diego. They will be returned to Guatemala unless they request and are granted asylum by an immigration judge.

5 The Asylum Seekers

In 1985, Sandra Salazar, her husband, two daughters — Wendy, ten, and Patty, eleven — and a younger son fled from their native Guatemala. Mrs. Salazar and her husband, Carlos, were teachers in a labor union, teaching members to read and write and also teaching them their rights as Guatemalan citizens. The oppressive, military-dominated government arrested Carlos, put him in a secret prison, and tortured him. Finally, with the help of the Catholic Church, he was released, but the family lived under constant threat of violence and death threats. In desperation, they escaped to Mexico.

They lived in Mexico City for two years, but after that time the Mexican government refused to renew their work permits and told them they would be returned to Guatemala. It was then that Mrs. Salazar and her husband decided to try to go to the United States with their children. In the 1980s, thousands of people like the Salazars fled the harsh, corrupt governments and internal warfare of the Central American countries of Guatemala, El Salvador, and Nicaragua. A number of churches and private homes on both sides of the U.S.-Mexican border formed a sanctuary movement, a kind of modern underground railroad, to help refugees evade the Border Patrol and enter the United States. Americans in the sanctuary movement were themselves breaking the law, and some were found guilty in court trials. But they felt they were carrying out a moral responsibility to help the persecuted people of Central America.

The Salazars were among the thousands of Central Americans helped across the border by the sanctuary movement. The Salazars began their new life in Tucson, an Arizona city with a large Hispanic population. Instead of living in fear and hiding as illegal aliens, the Salazars petitioned the Immigration and Naturalization Service for political asylum. They knew that they risked being deported to Guatemala if their request was denied, but they had the courage to take that risk.

THE United States has always been a haven for persons persecuted because of their political or religious beliefs. The Pilgrims, in Colonial America, were the first refugees to reach these shores. Since that time, millions of people have come to this country to escape tyranny and to be free to live according to their beliefs.

Almost a million Vietnamese, Cambodians, and Laotians have come to the United States from the refugee camps of Southeast Asia since the fall of South Vietnam to the North Vietnamese in 1975. Hundreds of thousands of Cubans have fled the Communist government of Fidel Castro, reaching the shores of south Florida in small, often unseaworthy, boats. Almost all have been given refugee status. Since the 1950s large numbers of Palestinians and Haitians also have come to the United States as refugees.

Sandra Salazar and her daughter Wendy in front of Maya Quetzal. Both Wendy and her sister, Patty, work in the restaurant when they can. Wendy goes to Pima Community College, and Patty works as a paralegal.

In 1988, Rafael fled with his family from El Salvador after two sons were killed by death squads. They were granted asylum, and Rafael went to live in Houston, where he worked as a painter and carpenter. Since the political situation has changed in El Salvador, the INS has told Rafael he must return to his country. Now seventy, he has asked the INS to reconsider its decision, but his future is uncertain.

A part of U.S. immigration law deals with refugees and defines a refugee as a person "who is unable or unwilling . . . to return to his country because of persecution on account of race, religion, or political opinion." Under this law, people anywhere in the world who are persecuted for political or religious reasons can petition the government for admission to the United States as a refugee.

Present immigration law limits the number of refugees who can enter the United States in any one year to 50,000. However, the law authorizes the president, in consultation with Congress, to raise the 50,000 ceiling as high as he believes necessary. In every year since 1980, the president has raised the ceiling, sometimes to well over 100,000. Refugees do not count against the limits of the number of regular immigrants who can be legally admitted to the country each year.

Persons given refugee status before they are brought to the United States (Vietnamese from the refugee camps of Asia, for example) usually are given permanent resident status just as if they were regular immigrants. But most people do not have the time or the means to go through the lengthy and complicated process of applying for refugee status before they come. They are running for their lives.

Even persons apprehended entering the United States illegally are entitled by law to a hearing before an immigration judge. Most Mexicans prefer to sign a voluntary return form, but thousands from other countries ask for a hearing. If the judge determines that a person is truly a refugee from persecution, he or she will be granted asylum in the United States and can get a work permit. Whether the person will become a permanent legal resident of the United States and be eligible to apply for citizenship

Alone and lonely in a detention center, this young Central American woman waits for her hearing for asylum.

will be decided by an immigration court later, sometimes years later. The decision may be based on political conditions in the country the person fled from.

MANY persons who are granted asylum become permanent legal residents and citizens and have good, productive lives in the United States. In many ways, the Salazars who entered the country as illegal aliens are almost storybook examples of a successful immigrant family in America. They were granted political asylum. Mrs. Salazar's husband found work in New Jersey, but she and the children stayed in Tucson. The children went to school. Mrs. Salazar got a job cleaning houses. She stayed closely in touch with the sanctuary groups that had helped her and her family. She helped new refugees become settled. She spoke to student groups and church groups. She told the story of her family's experience in Guatemala, and she began cooking for church and student groups — the good food of her native Guatemala.

One of the many friends Mrs. Salazar made in her church and student work was Rick Ufford-Chase, a young man who runs BorderLinks, an educational program about the U.S. frontier with Mexico. He suggested that, since she was spending so much of her time cooking Guatemalan food anyway, the two of them start a Guatemalan restaurant in Tucson.

The result was Maya Quetzal, the only Guatemalan restaurant in Arizona and one of the few anywhere in the United States. After two years the small, colorful restaurant is on its way to success. The good food and the authentic Guatemalan decorations have drawn favorable reviews not only from the local press but also from such out-of-state newspapers as *The Las Vegas*

Review-Journal and the prestigious *New York Times* in its travel section.

Considering their backgrounds, it is not surprising that Sandra Salazar and Rick Ufford-Chase have made a commitment to give 10 percent of the restaurant's profits to causes in Guatemala and 10 percent to homeless or immigrant programs in the United States. "Last year on the first anniversary of the restaurant, we gave $1,000 to an orphanage in Santa Palonia, Guatemala," Mrs. Salazar said.

The Salazars have been given permanent resident status and will apply for U.S. citizenship soon.

Rick Ufford-Chase (at right of chart on facing page) conducts a BorderLinks class. BorderLinks programs focus on U.S.-Mexican border concerns, and part of the time is spent in Mexico. The program grew out of the sanctuary movement and is funded by fees from attendees and some help from the Presbyterian Church. Rick feels that BorderLinks has changed a lot of people's thinking about the border. "And it has changed the direction of some lives."

The Border Watchers

WHEN THOUSANDS of uniformed men with guns — Border Patrol agents — try to stop millions of people from illegally crossing the border, some of those people are going to be hurt. A few will be shot when such deadly force was not needed. Some will be treated more roughly than necessary. Some people near the border who "look" Mexican or Hispanic may be detained as illegal aliens when they are not. Most of the violence will occur during moments of stress and bad judgment, but in some cases angry or frustrated agents will hit or push someone needlessly, or verbally abuse them, or commit other acts that cannot be excused.

Alleged abuses on the border are closely monitored and reported by several organizations. Among the most active are the Human Rights Watch/Americas and the American Friends Service Committee, which has an ongoing Immigration Law Enforcement Monitoring Project. Other more localized groups such as the Arizona Border Rights Project and the Human Rights Coalition of Arizona collect evidence of abuse of authority on the border in specific areas and, when possible, give aid to victims.

These border-watching organizations document cases of abuse as carefully as possible and report the results to the press, to Congress, and especially to the INS. Some of the organizations, particularly Human Rights Watch/Americas, complain that the INS does not pay enough attention to reports of unnecessary violence, some of which have resulted in court trials.

In response, the U.S. Attorney General and the INS Commissioner in 1994 established a citizen's advisory panel "to respond to concerns from private citizens, members of Congress, and organizations about allegations of human rights' abuses by INS employees." Committee members were chosen for their knowledge of human rights' issues and immigration; the committee held its first review meeting in 1995.

Members of Congress have also expressed their concern about excessive use of force and human rights' violations by the Border Patrol and customs inspectors. Congressman Xavier Becerra of California introduced the Immigration Law Enforcement Review Commission Act in 1993; the proposed legislation gained twenty-two members of Congress as cosponsors, but it was never voted on. Still, the INS is very much aware of Congress's concern.

Cases of excessive force and needless violence by border officials probably are small in relation to the millions of illegal border crossers. Nonetheless, the INS is well advised to take seriously any abuse of authority. A paragraph from a training manual studied by every Border Patrol agent explains why:

"The business of the United States Border Patrol is 'people.' These people come to the United States from all over the world. The Border Patrol agent may very well be an alien's first and only contact with an 'authority-figure' while in the United States, especially if he/she is apprehended shortly after entry. How these people are treated will leave a lasting impression of, not only the Border Patrol, but the United States in general."

Conditions like these in Mexican cities drive children across the border.

6 Into a Strange Land

Of ALL problems of illegal immigration, none is more troubling than that of children and teenagers who cross the border and try to make their way into the United States without a parent or other adult guardian. They come alone, some no older than eight, most in their teens. Many are homeless street children trying to escape a life of wretched poverty. Central American boys as young as eleven or twelve are fleeing army recruitment or death threats if they do not join antigovernment guerrilla forces. Others are escaping internal violence in Peru, Ecuador, and other South American countries.

Many of the children and teenagers from El Salvador, Guatemala, and Nicaragua are coming to find parents who fled to the United States to escape political persecution. Some of the young searchers have addresses, but most have only vague information about where their parents are. They have no idea how big the United States is. They do not speak or understand English.

The Border Patrol makes a special effort to apprehend young

illegal border crossers, for an unknown and possibly grim fate awaits them if they wander the streets and highways of the country. Mexican children apprehended can usually be returned immediately across the border, but children from other countries must be kept in detention until their cases are decided. They are really the lucky ones. Some of the detention centers leave much to be desired, and some of the detainees will be sent back to the country they came from. But for the others, the outcome will be good.

In Houston, Paul talked with one of the lucky ones, a fifteen-year-old girl named Dina. She had lived all her life in a small Guatemalan town with her father and mother and seven brothers and sisters. Her father is a farmer. Her mother became seriously ill and needed surgery, for which there was no money. Since her brothers and sisters are married and have their own responsibilities, Dina felt that she should go north to earn money for her mother's operation.

Dina swam a river to enter Mexico. She often slept in open fields and traveled north by canoe, bus, train, and on foot. After several weeks she reached Nuevo Laredo, the Mexican twin city of Laredo, Texas. She crossed the border into Texas and was caught almost immediately by the Border Patrol.

Because of her age, the INS sent Dina to Houston to live in a group home for young border crossers who have been apprehended by the Border Patrol. The group home is run by Catholic Charities of Houston, where the young detainees will receive the best of care until their cases have been decided. Dina has an aunt who lives in Miami, and investigation established that she could provide a good home for Dina. Immigration court decided that Dina could remain in the United States and live with her aunt.

When Dina heard that she would be talking to a photographer, she tied a red ribbon in her hair.

Arrangements have been made for Flavio to live in an apartment with another student and go to a Houston high school, where he will doubtless star on the school soccer team.

Dina is there now, where she can earn money for her mother and where she can go to school, which she wants very much to do.

In Houston, Paul also met Flavio Monteiro, a seventeen-year-old boy from Angola. Flavio was separated from his family during the terrible civil war in that African country. Because his father was being hunted by government troops, Flavio fled to South Africa, where he nearly starved as a homeless street boy. He stowed away on an American merchant ship and, when found, was turned over to immigration authorities in New Orleans. Flavio was granted political asylum and sent to Houston to live at Casa Juan Diego, a Catholic haven for undocumented men, women, and children. A good student and gifted soccer player, Flavio was recently named to the all-Houston soccer team.

No COMPLETE figures are kept on the number of children and teenagers apprehended crossing the border into the United States, and no one knows how many elude the Border Patrol or what happens to them afterward. But the Tucson Ecumenical Council Legal Assistance Project (TECLA), a church-related organization that helps young illegal border crossers, keeps its own figures. They are disturbing because they reveal a sharp rise in the number of unaccompanied boys and girls from Central and South America who are trying to enter the United States through Arizona. In 1993, TECLA was called on to assist 132 boys and girls caught by the Border Patrol and put in detention. In the first nine months of 1994 that figure rose to 320.

When Paul and I visited the small, dedicated TECLA staff, they were struggling with a backlog of over 200 pending juvenile

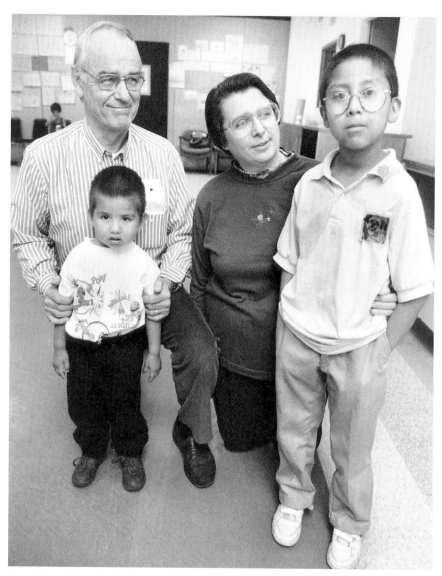

Mark and Louise Zwick established Casa Juan Diego, a Catholic haven in Houston for undocumented border crossers. At least 10 percent of those coming for help are under the age of eighteen. The two children shown here belong to a battered woman from Mexico who sought refuge at Casa Juan Diego. The boy with glasses was almost totally blind from a rare eye condition and the Zwicks arranged for eye surgery.

cases. Federal immigration law permits some illegal entrants under the age of eighteen to remain in the United States if they can join responsible relatives living in the United States. Others may be allowed to stay if it can be proved that returning to their home country would not be in their best interests and if a foster home can be found for them in the United States.

TECLA represents children in detention in immigration court hearings, locates relatives living in the United States, finds foster homes, arranges transportation to join relatives or to go to foster homes. Catholic Charities in Houston gives similar help to boys and girls whose lives of desperation have driven them across the border.

"They're at the mercy of so many people along the way," says Marcy Jones, a lawyer for TECLA.

The U.S. Hispanic population, now exceeding 25 million, is not confined to the Southwest. Hispanic festivals such as this one in Herndon, Virginia, are held throughout the country to celebrate the contributions of food, music, art, and other aspects of Latin American culture to the United States. (Jennifer Ashabranner)

7 Illegal Immigration: Where Do We Go From Here?

THE problem of illegal immigration cannot be solved in the foreseeable future. It is too complex and affected by too many conditions over which the United States has limited control or no control. But there are decisions we can make, actions we can take, and understandings we can reach that will make the problem more manageable and in time lessen it.

First, we must continue vigorous enforcement of our immigration laws. Our enforcement program isn't perfect, and it never will be; but it is working, and it will work better if it continues to get the support it needs. The Border Patrol's morale is high, and there are enough agents on duty now for it to be more effective than it has ever been. Future budget plans call for adding another 2,000 agents, which will put the Border Patrol at prime strength for doing its job. The INS should continue its vigorous fight against document fraud and step up its deportation of aliens in detention, particularly those who have committed crimes.

ENFORCEMENT of our immigration laws is basic, but enforcement isn't everything. As a nation we need to understand the realities of illegal immigration better than we do now and take action on our improved understanding. A fundamental understanding is that we shouldn't panic. We are not being "overwhelmed" by "hordes" of illegals. If there are 4 million illegal immigrants in the United States (probably a top estimate), that is only about 1.5 percent of our national population of 260 million. We must keep trying in every reasonable way to reduce the country's illegal population, but 1.5 percent is not a figure that should frighten us.

We should also remember that the United States is not alone with its problems of illegal immigration. France, Germany, and other European countries have problems with large numbers of immigrants — many of whom are illegal immigrants — from Turkey, Algeria, and other countries of Africa and Asia. South Africa, a relatively prosperous country, has been unable to stem the illegal migrant influx from neighboring Mozambique and other African countries with severe problems of failing economies and overpopulation.

Nor is the United States alone in receiving refugees. The United Nations High Commissioner for Refugees estimates that in 1995 there are 23 million refugees in the world. The United States has been generous in the share of the problem it assumes, but the problem of refugees troubles all parts of the world.

The concentration of illegal immigrants in a few states is a very real problem, and those states — particularly California, Texas, and Florida — are justified in looking to the federal government for help with education, health, and other costs.

Immigration is a federal responsibility. Fortunately, the president and Congress know this, and the signs are good that the states concerned will receive help.

Perhaps more than anything, we should strive for a better understanding of Mexico. In an article in *The Washington Post* former Assistant Secretary of State for Latin-American Affairs William D. Rogers explained why we should: "If the United States has one truly special relationship with another country, that country is Mexico. A nation can choose its friends, but not its neighbors. We and Mexico are fated to live together. . . . We had best learn to exist side by side, with civility and understanding. What injures Mexico does damage to our own national interests as well."

How can we give the specialness of Mexico concrete form as it concerns illegal immigrants? Perhaps we should consider sharply raising the annual number of immigrant visas available to Mexicans. Perhaps we should consider a new kind of guestworker program with Mexico, especially for the border area; we have had successful guestworker programs with Mexico in the past. We should certainly streamline the issuance of border crossing cards for visiting relatives and conducting business here.

The North American Free Trade Agreement (NAFTA), ratified by Congress in 1994, recognizes the special relationship between the United States, Mexico, and Canada. Proponents of the agreement believe that it will reduce illegal immigration by creating hundreds of thousands of new jobs in Mexico. Others, however, believe that dislocations caused by NAFTA will, at least for the short run, increase illegal immigration. Only time and the close monitoring of how the NAFTA agreement works will provide the answer.

Abelardo, a Nicaraguan boy, was kidnapped and forced into the army by the Sandinista military regime when he was thirteen years old. He fled to the United States, was apprehended by the Border Patrol at Nogales, and was given political asylum.

WITH its emphasis on family reunification and acceptance of refugees from political and religious persecution, our national immigration policy is based in large measure on compassion. Compassion should also be a part of our policy in dealing with illegal immigrants. Fortunately, it already is, with its procedures for letting asylum seekers make their cases and for giving special consideration and help to unaccompanied children and teenagers who cross the border illegally. The huge backlog of asylum cases needs attention, and many more facilities are needed to house young people while their cases are being decided. But our policy is on the right track.

And what of Proposition 187? The frustration that inspired it is understandable, but surely there is a better way than denying education, health care, and food to children. It is hard not to agree with *New York Times* columnist William Safire when he wrote of Proposition 187, ". . . in terms of practicality and of the American spirit, a government policy of making any child's life miserable is still an abomination."

ENFORCEMENT. Understanding. Compassion. If we build a policy based on those elements, we can deal successfully with the very real problems that illegal immigration presents. And the United States will continue to be what it has always been: the most open, the most accessible, the friendliest country in the world.

Border Patrol agents bringing illegal border crossers out of Trickey Wash, Nogales.

United States Immigration Law and Selection System

For ALMOST a hundred years after nationhood, immigration to the United States was completely unrestricted. Anyone with the will and the means could come here to live. But as the country developed and its population grew, laws controlling the immigrant influx became necessary. The laws have gone through many changes since the first immigration law was passed in 1882, and changes continue to be debated in every session of Congress. U.S. immigration law today is very complex with scores of provisions, but the main elements are these:

— No person can be refused immigrant status because of race, nationality, or religion.

— Preference in issuing immigration visas will be shown for
   1. family-sponsored immediate relatives of U.S. citizens and legally resident noncitizens
   2. persons with special occupational and professional skills that will be useful in the United States

3. persons from "underrepresented" countries, the countries to be determined annually and total visas limited to 55,000 in this preference category

— The annual limit on immigration is set each year by Congress, but there is some flexibility in the cap or ceiling. The limit in 1994 was 755,000. Limits are set on all of the above preference categories.

— Minor children and parents of legal immigrants do not count against the immigration limit.

— Up to 50,000 refugees from political or religious persecution in their homeland can be admitted annually. This limit can be raised by the president in consultation with Congress. Refugees do not count against the immigration limit.

A Note on Information Sources

Unless otherwise cited, all figures in this book having to do with illegal immigration were supplied by the INS Statistics Division, Office of Policy and Planning. All figures and other information regarding the official United States Immigration program were obtained from the INS Public Affairs Office or from studies produced by the Population Reference Bureau, a nonprofit research and public information organization in Washington, D.C. These studies are listed in the bibliography.

Information about the work of the United States Coast Guard in interdicting persons attempting to enter the United States illegally was furnished by the Coast Guard Public Affairs Office. The U.S. Office of International Boundary and Water Commission in El Paso furnished information on the length of the U.S.-Mexican border in its entirety and its various state segments. The Canadian Embassy provided information on the length of the U.S.-Canadian border.

Bibliography

Ashabranner, Brent. *Dark Harvest: Migrant Farmworkers in America.* New York: Dodd, Mead & Co., 1985. (Reissued by Linnet Books, Hamden, Conn., 1993.)

_____. *The New Americans: Changing Patterns in U.S. Immigration.* New York: Dodd, Mead & Co., 1983.

_____. *Still a Nation of Immigrants.* New York: Cobblehill Books, 1993.

_____. *The Vanishing Border: A Photographic Journey Along Our Frontier with Mexico.* New York: Dodd, Mead & Co., 1987.

Bennett, William J. "Immigration: Making Americans." *The Washington Post,* December 4, 1994.

Bouvier, Leon F. and Robert W. Gardner. "Immigration to the U.S.: The Unfinished Story." *Population Bulletin,* Vol. 41, No. 4, November, 1986. (Population Reference Bureau, Washington, D.C.)

Brimelow, Peter. *Alien Nation: Common Sense About America's Immigration Disaster.* New York: Random House, 1995.

Brooks, Laura. "INS Discovers 1 Arizona Worker in 10 Is Illegal." *The Arizona Daily Star,* February 21, 1995.

Church, George J. "Mexico's Troubles Are Our Troubles." *Time,* March 6, 1995.

Claiborne, William. "A Moving Challenge on the Border." *The Washington Post,* May 26, 1995.

"Crossing the Line." New York: Human Rights Watch/Americas, 1995. (A report on human rights abuses on the U.S.-Mexican border.)

Davis, Cary, Carl Haub, JoAnne Willette. "U.S. Hispanics: Changing the Face of America." *Population Bulletin,* Vol. 38, No. 3, June, 1983. (Population Reference Bureau, Washington, D.C.)

Duke, Lynne. "South Africa Fails to Stem Migrant Influx." *The Washington Post,* August 16, 1995.

Fuchs, Lawrence H. *The American Kaleidoscope: Race, Ethnicity, and the Civic Culture.* Hanover, N.H., and London:University Press of New England (Wesleyan University Press), 1990.

Hoagland, Jim. "Illegal Immigrants: Not Just California's Problem." *The Washington Post,* October 30, 1994.

Kissinger, Henry. "Why We Can't Give Up on Mexico." *The Washington Post,* April 22, 1995.

Martin, Philip and Elizabeth Midgley. "Immigration to the United States: Journey to an Uncertain Destination." *Population Bulletin,* Vol. 49, No. 2, September, 1994. (Population Reference Bureau, Washington, D.C.)

Martin, Philip. "Proposition 187 in California." *International Migration Review,* Spring, 1995.

Mathews, Jessica. "Immigration and the Press of the Poor." *The Washington Post,* November 21, 1994.

Martinez, Oscar J. *Border People: Life and Society in the U.S.-Mexico Borderlands.* Tucson: University of Arizona Press, 1994.

"Operation Blockade: A City Divided." Philadelphia: American Friends Service Committee, July, 1994. (A report about the Border Patrol's operations in El Paso.)

Sanders, Ron. "Challenge on the Border." *The Tucson Citizen*, July 1, 1995.

"Sealing Our Borders: The Human Toll." Philadelphia: American Friends Service Committee, February, 1992. (Third report of the Immigration Law Enforcement Monitoring Project.)

Simon, Julian L. *The Economic Consequences of Immigration*. Cambridge, Mass.: Basil Blackwell, Inc., 1989. (Published in association with the Cato Institute.)

Index

Becerra, Xavier, 73

Bennett, William J., 10

BorderLinks, 69, 71

Border Patrol, U.S.
    annual budget, 11
    Nogales, Arizona, activities
      (Operation Safeguard),
      29-31, 33-39
    number of agents in service
      in 1995, 42
    selection and training of
      agents, 42-43

Calvert, H.M. (Mike), 45-46

Casa Juan Diego, 79, 80

Casteneda, Mario, 49

Castro, Fidel, 46-47

Coast Guard, U.S., 56-59

Franken, Mark, *xi*

Guttierez, David, 37-39

Illegal immigrants
    amnesty conditions, 48, 49
    children and teenagers as,
      75-81
    concentration in California
      and other states, 11, 51,
      53, 84-85
    national resentment of, 47-
      48, 50-51, 53, 54
    number from Mexico, 9
    number settling in United

States each year, 9
total in United States, 9
Immigration Reform and
Control Act of 1986
(IRCA), 48

Kennedy, Edward (Senator),
48
Knowles, Ken, 43

Maquiladoras, 22-25
Mariel, Cuba, 46-47
"Marielitos," 47
McDonald, Steve, 29-31, 33,
35
Meissner, Doris M., 61
Mexico
bracero program, 20
economic conditions
encouraging immigration
to United States, 17, 21
interdependence with
United States, 85

North American Free Trade
Agreement (NAFTA), 85

Oaks, Kevin, 41

Proposition 187 (California),
47, 51, 53, 87

Refugees
as asylum seekers, 63-64,
66
definition, 67
sanctuary movement, 63-
65
United States law concern-
ing, 67, 69
Rogers, William D., 85

Safire, William, 87
Salazar, Sandra, 63-64, 65,
69-70
Salcido, Pablo, 55
Sojourners (nonimmigrant
illegal aliens), 9

Tucson Ecumenical Council
Legal Assistance Project
(TECLA), 79, 81

Ufford-Chase, Rick, 69-70,
71
U.S.-Canadian border, 26-27
U.S. Immigration and Natur-

alization Service (INS)
    document fraud investiga-
      tions, 48, 60-61
    monitoring human rights
      violations, 72-73

U.S.-Mexican border
    boundary fence, 15, 33, 34

characteristics of, 15-17
closeness of border rela-
    tionships, 54-55
length, 15

Visa abusers, 8-9

Zwick, Mark and Louise, 80